M000014689

WISDOM

on America

RICHARD C. HALVERSON

VISION™
HOUSE
PUBLISHING, INC.
Gresham, Oregon 97030

WISDOM ON AMERICA
© 1994 by Richard C. Halverson

Published by Vision House Publishing, Inc.

Edited by Chip MacGregor
Cover Design by Multnomah Graphics
Interior Design by Martin Bogan

Printed in the United States of America

International Standard Book Number: 1-885305-10-9

Vision House Publishing, Inc.
1217 N.E. Burnside Road, Suite 403
Gresham, Oregon 97030

Scripture references are from:

New American Standard Bible, The Lockman Foundation © 1960, 1962, 1963, 1968, 1971, 1972, 1973, 1975, 1977. Used by permission.

New International Version, © 1973, 1978, 1984 by International Bible Society. Used by permission of Zondervan Publishing House.

All rights reserved. The "NIV" and "New International Version" trademarks are registered in the United States Patent and Trademark Office by International Bible Society. Use of either trademark requires the permission of International Bible Society.

Revised Standard Version of the Bible, © 1946, 1952, 1971, 1973, Division of Christian Education, National Council of Churches of Christ in the USA. Used by permission.

J. B. Phillips: The New Testament in Modern English, J. B. Phillips © 1958. Used by permission of Macmillan Publishing Co., Inc.

The Good News Bible in Today's English Version, © 1983. Used by permission of Thomas Nelson, Inc.

 94 95 96 97 98 99 00 01 02 03 — 10 9 8 7 6 5 4 3 2 1

e the people of the United States...

"In order to form a more perfect union, establish justice, insure domestic tranquillity, provide for the common defense, promote the general welfare, and secure the blessings of liberty to ourselves and our posterity...

"Do ordain and establish this Constitution for the United States of America."

What an incredible statement!

What a revolutionary concept in its time - a sovereign people ordaining their government.

Where did it come from?

The Bible!

God gave *sovereignty to the people*...

Any system which violates this principle built into history triggers the forces of self-destruction. Sovereignty belongs to the people.

But the people repudiate their sovereignty if they *refuse to govern themselves.* They may delegate authority to their representatives…

But they may not abdicate without forfeiting their sovereignty.

Non-involvement of the people in the democratic processes shaped by our Constitution means that they reject their sovereignty.

Furthermore, the people's sovereignty is derived - it is not absolute. God ordained it and it works only as the people acknowledge the Source of their sovereignty and submit to the rule of God.

When man turns from God he opens the flood gates to the tyranny of vested interests - oligarchies and dictatorships in many forms.

God or tyranny… the people's alternatives!

"But if serving the Lord seems undesirable to you, then choose for yourselves this day whom you will serve, whether the gods your forefathers served, or the gods of the Amorites, in whose land you are living. But as for me and my household, we will serve the Lord."

— *Joshua 24:15*

Four score and seven years ago our fathers brought forth, upon this continent, a new nation, conceived in Liberty and dedicated to the proposition that all men are created equal... "

These unforgettable words which for years, if not at present, were learned by every student in a public school, are *profound in their simplicity*.

President Lincoln, of course, referred to the Declaration of Independence. "We hold these truths to be self evident that all men are created equal... " The basis for our political system.

After 75 years of watching atheistic Communism, which throttled, punished, and destroyed every semblance of human liberty, why is it so difficult for us in America to realize that *liberty is the gift of God; that Godlessness is destructive of liberty*.

What's really happening in America is that, having eliminated God for all practical purposes from our thinking, secular society, we have *reduced liberty to license*. License is fast becoming *total anarchy*.

In our preoccupation with materialism we have forsaken freedom, of which order is a prerequisite. We have eliminated order, or law, and opened the door to total moral and ethical relativism.

Inevitably, tyrants emerge out of social anarchy.

As President Lincoln concluded his brief remarks, he said to those gathered at Gettysburg: "... that we here highly resolve that these dead shall not have died in vain; that this nation under God shall have a new birth of freedom; and that this government of the people, by the people, for the people, shall not perish from the earth."

"He looked for justice, but saw bloodshed; for righteousness, but heard cries of distress."

— *Isaiah 5:7b*

This magnificent accident," thus a business executive referred to America in a service club address. Could he have meant what he said? Could an intelligent businessman actually believe that?

Is it possible a man can be so blinded to the facts of American heritage? Have we been so completely cut off from our historical roots?

Nothing could be further from the truth!

America is not an accident. America — its way of life, its unsurpassed liberty and prosperity — these are not accidental. *They are the unquestionable result of Biblical Christianity and the church.*

India is a product of her religion: poverty, beggars by the thousands, child brides, sacred cows. China is a product of her religion: poverty, tyranny, unhappiness. *These things result logically*, inevitably when men forsake the true God, refuse the Bible, and reject Jesus Christ.

America at her best: the Bill of Rights, liberty, prosperity, dignity, free enterprise, private ownership of property... *everything worthwhile about America is due to belief in the Bible!* Former President Coolidge said, "America was born in a revival of religion."

Daniel Webster, who read the Bible through each year, once wrote: "If we abide by the principles taught in the Bible, our country will go on prospering and to prosper. *But if we and our posterity neglect its instruction and authority,* no man can tell how sudden a catastrophe may overwhelm us." America's strength depends upon her righteousness before God.

A visiting Chinese professor put it this way: "I have studied all the great religions of the world. When I came to study the Bible and Jesus, I found in Him all the truth of other religions *and so much more besides* that if I can only take Christ back to China - China will be saved."

"The fear of the Lord is the beginning of wisdom."

— *Proverbs 9:10*

Self government...

The *foundation* of American greatness.

Unique among the nations of history - providing the greatest good for the largest number and the longest time...

Despite many gross failures.

"We the people... "

The words which begin our national constitution.

"Government of the people - by the people - and for the people." Fantastic!

But self government means *self* government!

It means accountability to order, to other people, and to the common good.

It is the antithesis of selfishness... in direct opposition to the "me first" policy.

At its heart it means self-discipline and social responsibility.

It means taking justice and truth and integrity seriously.

Abdication from personal responsibility is the poison of self government... its end: decay and disintegration.

Fundamentally it means *accountability to God!*

Self government is God's idea! To forsake God is to surrender self government to certain doom. A godless society generates anarchy or tyranny.

"In those days Israel had no king; everyone did what was right in his own eyes."

— Judges 17:6

We hold these truths to be self evident...

(That is *indisputable truth!*)

"That all men are created equal - and that they are endowed by their Creator with certain unalienable rights...

(That is *inviolable rights!*)

"To secure these rights governments are instituted among men, deriving their just powers from the consent of the governed."

(That is *a sovereign people!*)

A sovereign people - *from which government gets its authority and its mandate...* to secure human rights which are sacrosanct.

That's what America's independence is all about!

Take Creator God out of the formula — *the whole structure collapses!*

Get rid of God… you get rid of democracy.

The framers of the Declaration of Independence had their priorities straight.

Our founding fathers knew the foundation upon which they built our Constitutional form of government.

The order: *God, the ultimate Authority*. Man, accountable to God - His partner in governing the world - in charge of his environment.

Remove man's accountability to God, open the door to anarchy, which ushers in tyranny — and man becomes a victim of his environment.

"So God created man in His own image… male and female He created them. And God blessed them, and God said to them, 'Be fruitful and multiply, and fill the earth and subdue it; and have dominion over the fish of the sea and over the birds of the air and over every living thing *that* moves upon the earth.' "

— *Genesis 1:27-28*

All that must happen for evil to prevail is for good men to do nothing."

— Edmund Burke

Absenteeism at the polls is *unpardonable for the follower of Christ.*

Choices are rarely the best or the worst...

Often it is the lesser of two evils... Or the better of two goods.

Not uncommonly, opposite extremes are closer together than those on either side but closer to center.

We live in a sinful world...

All worldly systems are infinitely less than God's best.

None passes through into eternity as the perfect way.

God's kingdom, God's will, God's plan for eternity is utterly different than the best system devised by man.

But we live in this world…

We are a part of it…

We are meant to assume our responsibility as members of the community.

Copping out is unbecoming the servant of Christ.

Being involved is of the very essence of "incarnation."

We are to be Christ's representatives - Christ's presence - indeed Christ's body in the world.

Each has the right to vote as he pleases — the private polling booth is at the heart of the democratic process

But each has the responsibility to vote!

"Render unto Caesar the things that are Caesar's."

— *Matthew 22:21*

We've come a long way from the principle of "inalienable rights" for which our forebears risked their "lives, their fortunes and their sacred honor."

Human rights have degenerated into "I can do as I please," or "If it feels good, do it."

Our ancestors laid down their lives for human rights... we've made them "payable on demand."

Freedom has been reduced to license.

Responsibility is a forgotten word, as is the God who endowed humans with their rights.

In our passion to legislate rights, we forget that the authority which grants rights has the power to revoke them.

God-given rights are inalienable and no power on earth has the authority to abrogate them.

Indeed, in the minds of those who founded our nation, government existed to preserve inalienable rights...

And it ruled "with the consent of the governed."

No God, no inalienable rights... *government moves from the position of protecting rights to the position of granting rights.*

Rights are up for grabs. They come by lobbying — or demonstrating — or protesting.

What incredible wisdom: "We hold these truths to be self-evident, that all men are created equal; that they are endowed by their Creator with certain inalienable rights... To secure these rights governments are instituted among men, deriving their just powers from the consent of the governed."

"You are all sons of God through faith in Christ Jesus... there is neither Jew nor Greek, slave nor free, male nor female, for you are all one in Christ Jesus."

— *Galatians 3:26-27*

8

Having spent three weeks in Europe, besieged with the criticism of U.S. "imperialism", I want to record a few simple facts of history.

At the end of World War II, *the great cities of Europe and Japan were in ruins* — their lands ravaged — their factories rubble — their people exhausted.

The USA had been spared war on her soil. Her cities were thriving — her factories geared to maximum production - her people were eager, their morale never higher.

She had the most powerful army, navy and air force in history... deployed throughout the world - a powerful occupation force.

And she alone had the atomic bomb!

The United States was in position literally to take over the world — an unprecedented imperialistic opportunity!

What would the Soviet Union have done in that position? Germany? Japan? The question, of course, is hypothetical…

But what the United States did is not. The record stands!

She retooled for peace. She joined hands with people everywhere to rebuild the world — not parsimoniously, but magnanimously, spontaneously, humbly.

She poured her industrial, agricultural, and financial might into Europe, Asia, Latin America and Africa… billions and billions of dollars in aid and redevelopment" She put the world back on its feet. *How easily we forget!*

The world is in the United States today. Every nation on earth is represented among her people… and millions from other nations seek refuge in her borders.

"Our Father's God to Thee, Author of liberty, to Thee we sing.

Long may our land be bright, with freedom's holy light,

Protect us by Thy might, Great God our King."

Why do empires and nations fall from power? Why do they decline and collapse?

History is replete with evidence that *no great empire was defeated from without before it had rotted from within, spiritually, morally and ethically.*

The Roman Empire certainly did not collapse for lack of military power. Rome had no match militarily - but she fell!

It was fatally vulnerable to the fierce forces without because of its materialism, hedonism and self-indulgence — its amoral, permissive social decay within.

America is no exception!

She will never be destroyed by forces from without but from her own decadence.

America's need is critical for a spiritual, moral, ethical re-birth.

That will never come until the church becomes the Church again…

Until Christians become Christian!

As long as professed followers of Christ are indistinguishable from the culture around them, there is no reason to expect that the nation will be saved from secular, materialistic, hedonistic suicide… *unless we turn to God in repentance and call on His name.*

"If my people, which are called by my name, shall humble themselves, and pray, and seek my face, and turn from their wicked ways; then will I hear from heaven, and will forgive their sin, and will heal their land."

— 2 Chronicles 7:14

Righteousness is a social word!

It is more than personal morality and piety...

It has to do with relationship.

Righteousness is right relationship with God, with others, and with self.

Righteousness and justice are identical in the Bible.

Righteousness is justice — justice is righteousness!

Fundamentally it has to do with stewardship; our use of that with which we have been entrusted by God.

Life — breath — health — strength — aptitude — talent — ability — possessions — place — potential — freedom — choice — will — To waste or abuse these endowments, or to consume them selfishly, is to be unrighteous and unjust.

It is to live *in violation of* God's order and God's love.

One may be moral and ethical and pious... and at the same time be unrighteous and unjust.

Righteousness (justice) is *to take seriously the two great commandments:* love God with all one's being and love one's neighbor as oneself.

Jesus tells us in Matthew 5:6, "Blessed are they that hunger and thirst after righteousness, they shall be satisfied." In that same sermon, He said, "Seek first the kingdom of God and its justice."

— Matthew 6:33

Justice is a social word! We will experience it as a nation when we determine to love God and our fellow man.

"I am not ashamed of the gospel of Christ for it is the power of God unto salvation to everyone who believes, to the Jew first and also to the Greek... for therein is the justice of God revealed."

— Romans 1:16-17

Things are not good or bad *in and of themselves*...

It is *the touch of man* that makes the difference.

In our human pride we refuse to acknowledge this,

And blame inanimate things for our dilemma.

Nuclear energy is neither moral nor immoral...

It's how man uses it.

It's in vogue today to blame the system — whatever is meant by that.

But systems are neutral, becoming evil or good depending upon how men use them.

Of course, some systems are better than others.

Dictatorship is the most efficient political system...

But where do you find a benevolent dictator?

Democracy is slow and inefficient - but it guarantees the greatest freedom and opportunity for the greatest number.

You don't get 100 percent saints in public office... But you don't get all devils either!

Whether it's democracy or dictatorship, the system is good or evil, depending on the men who run it.

Evil men will use any system for evil purposes...

And nobody disputes the fact that this is happening to our system today. .

The answer is not to change the system - but to change the men who run it.

Good men will use the system for benevolent purposes.

Jesus Christ said, "He that would be greatest, let him be the servant of all."

— *Matthew 20:26*

More than two hundred years ago, Gibbon completed his monumental work, *The Decline and Fall of the Roman Empire*, recognized as the classic on the disintegration, decay and demise of Rome, in which were listed five reasons for the catastrophic end of the great Roman Empire:

"1. The rapid increase in divorce — *undermining the dignity and sanctity of the home* which is the basis of human society;

2. Higher and higher taxes — the spending of *public monies for free bread and circuses*;

3. The *mad craze for pleasure* — sports becoming every year more exciting and more brutal;

4. The building of *gigantic armaments* — when the real enemy was within, the decadence of the people;

5. The decay of religion — *faith fading into a mere form*, losing touch with life and becoming impotent to guide the people."

The last reason contains the clue to all the others. The first four are effects... the last is the cause. Reason number five is the root of which the first four are the fruit.

Divorce, undermining of the home, pleasure-mad people, and moral decadence are symptoms... symptoms of the fact that men have turned from the living and true God.

In 1949, with piercing diagnosis, the editors of *Life* magazine said, "The worst enemy western civilization faces is not communism. The worst enemy is within our civilization. Our sixty-four dollar euphemism for it is secularism. A blunter word is Godlessness."

Godlessness. Whether you call it by its right name or by another, it is at the root of the disintegration of any people or nation. Godlessness is not atheism! *Godlessness is to live without regard for God, His will, His plan!*

The cure is obvious! We must turn to God, give Him His place in our lives... and make the choice! Christ or chaos!

"Righteousness exalteth a nation... sin is a reproach to any people."

— *Proverbs 14:34*

"**C**ongress shall make no law respecting an establishment of religion or prohibiting the free exercise thereof."

Two clauses — the first of which has been a preoccupation of those who insist that our government be secular...

Not just nonreligious — *but antireligious!*

Think about this...

What about the second clause?

"Congress shall make no law... prohibiting the free exercise" (of religion).

No mention of when or where!

It doesn't say "free exercise of religion in public schools or public places, etc., etc."

Simply: There are to be no laws prohibiting the free exercise of religion.

How about some litigation over this?

An interesting dilemma — enforcing the first clause — violating the second.

Our founding fathers were endorsing a government neutral toward religion, *not the absence of it or opposition to it.*

"We hold these truths to be self-evident, that all men are created equal, that they are endowed by their Creator with certain unalienable Rights, that among these are Life, Liberty, and the Pursuit of Happiness. That to secure these Rights, Governments are instituted among Men, deriving their just Powers from the Consent of the Governed."

⚞ 14 ⚟

As you enter the Jefferson Memorial from the Tidal Basin, inscribed on the wall to your right is a paragraph from the *Declaration of Independence*:

"We hold these truths to be self-evident that all men are created equal, that they are endowed by their Creator with certain unalienable Rights, that among these are Life, Liberty and the pursuit of Happiness. That to secure these rights, Governments are instituted among Men, deriving their just powers from the consent of the governed…"

As you leave the memorial, the wall to your right contains another paragraph which begins with two very penetrating sentences.

First, *"God who gave us life gave us liberty."*

The second sentence is a haunting question:

"Can the liberties of a nation be secure if we have removed from the hearts of the people the belief that those liberties are the gift of God?"

Those profound sentences reflect the convictions of our founding fathers who drafted the Bill of Rights which our government is to "secure."

Is it possible that, at a time when millions of oppressed people are sacrificing for their "God given rights", that we in America, because of our Godless, secular thinking, are forfeiting those rights?

"Take heed lest you forget the Lord your God... lest, when you have eaten and are full, and have built goodly houses and live in them, and when your herds and flocks multiply, and your silver and gold is multiplied, and all that you have is multiplied, then your heart be lifted up, and you forget the Lord your God... Beware lest you say in your heart, 'My power and the might of my hand have gotten me this wealth'... And if you forget the Lord your God and go after other gods and serve them and worship them, I solemnly warn you this day that you shall surely perish. Like the nations that the Lord makes to perish before you, so shall you perish, because you would not obey the voice of the Lord your God."

— *Deuteronomy 8:11,12-14,17,19-20 RSV*

15

The perfect government.

One of the deepest longings of the human heart is a government which will rule in perfect freedom, justice and equity.

Implicit in every political party's platform — in every political campaign — is the promise that the peoples' desire for a perfect government will be realized.

It is the preoccupation of America every four years.

Despite which the perfect government has never been realized in more than 200 years of American history — nor in all the years of recorded human history.

In fact, year by year, cynicism grows — people become more and more embittered by political systems, and expect less and less.

Is hope for the perfect government futile? Is this universal dream never to be realized — a fantasy which has no foundation in reality?

The answer is a resounding NO! This stubborn, fundamental, persistent demand of the human heart will have its fulfillment!

This is the legacy of Christ's birth.

God's plan for history includes the perfect government. Indeed, He planted the desire in the human heart at creation. In the divine economy history will be consummated in this perfection.

Which certifies the abolition of every evil which today infects human society.

Christ is the promise of the perfect social order — the answer to the highest human aspirations throughout all generations.

God plans "in the fullness of time to unite all things in Christ."

— Ephesians 1:10

"... of the increase of His government and of peace there will be no end."

— Isaiah 9:7

16

Democracy doesn't work without the Bible!

We take its roots for granted — we assume democracy will work anywhere like it works here.

We are frustrated by its failure in emerging independent nations; perplexed by the ease with which dictatorships or autocracies take over.

We suffer the illusion that "self-determination" is a passion with people everywhere. Nothing could be further from the truth!

The fact is, the concept of self-determination is a product of the Judeo-Christian tradition received from the Bible.

Our Western world has been immersed in this tradition for centuries. In the words of a leading American, it is "in our bloodstream."

It was *the deepest conviction of the founders of the oldest democratic republic in the world* — and they engraved it on the cornerstone of America.

The very heart and soul of democracy is the inherent dignity of man and the supreme worth of the individual. That's an exclusively Biblical concept! It is foreign to non-Biblical cultures.

They try to copy democracy, to imitate what the West has been doing for centuries. And it simply doesn't work. They have the theory without the substance. They get the idea but there's no heart in it. The experiment collapses on the concept of man.

Human value and dignity eludes them... concern for the "common good" is as rare as snow in July in cultures where the Judeo-Christian tradition has relatively little impact.

Legislation cannot dismiss in a generation what non-Biblical culture has been maturing for centuries.

Not that we should capitulate to tyranny — nor desist from exporting freedom and democracy to the extent that their precepts and example will be accepted.

But we ought to be realists, recognize the roots from whence we came, and export those principles and concepts without which democracy is an illusion.

The Bible is indispensable! Let's take it seriously.

"Your statutes are my heritage forever; they are the joy of my heart."

— *Psalm 119:111*

Here is an exceedingly prophetic utterance made many years ago at a conference in Noordwijk, Holland, by Dr. Gerhard Schroeder, then Federal Minister of the Interior, West Germany, later Chairman of Foreign Relations in the Parliament:

"It was the stimulating conviction of our grandfathers that civilization on the basis of technical progress was bound to lead to permanent improvement of the world and finally to a happy solution of all its problems.

A few thinkers tried to criticize this optimism as naive. Today they seem to us great prophets who anticipated the present crisis.

More and more, philosophers, historians, and poets of the different nations have pointed out that belief in the progress of the world is an error.

The political events, the social revolutions, and the confusion of philosophical thought at the present time have confirmed these pessimistic prophecies.

The optimism of the past has turned into dark pessimism."

More than four decades have passed since that statement was made in 1954 and the cumulative experience has served to confirm the "dark pessimism."

Not only are we not solving our human problems, they are compounding: crime, drug abuse, alcoholism, divorce, terrorism, child abuse, wife abuse, etc., etc.

We have become technological giants… *and moral adolescents.*

Our progress in ethics and morals and humanness has declined in inverse proportion to our technical and scientific expertise.

Man is truly human only as he is rightly related to God. Sin is man's self-alienation from God.

Jesus Christ came into history to redeem man… that is to restore man's relationship with God.

"Be ye reconciled to God."

— *II Corinthians 5:20*

—ull. 18 ℩mo—

If there were only two alternatives, which would you choose?

(1) Continuing and *growing economic prosperity* free from threat of recession, inflation or depression…

with *declining morality* and ethics — injustice, violence, oppression and inhumanity?

Or…

(2) *Economic uncertainty with spiritual renewal*, pervasive morality and ethical reformation together with a revival of authentic faith?

Of course, we are not reduced to those two alternatives but the fact is that one senses in some of the urgency for national repentance an undeclared presupposition that such repentance would guarantee prosperity.

In other words — spiritual renewal is in order to economic abundance. Which is, to say the least, an unworthy reason for desiring national humiliation and repentance.

Indeed, it is conceivable that our very preoccupation with our own comfort and ease and prosperity; our addiction to materialism; our presuming upon the extraordinary benefits God has so graciously bestowed upon us as a people... it is conceivable that these are the very things of which we must repent.

In the words of Abraham Lincoln (April 1863), "We have grown in numbers, wealth, and power as no other nation has grown — *but we have forgotten God.*

We have forgotten the gracious hand that preserved us in peace, and multiplied and enriched and strengthened us...

We have vainly imagined that all these blessings were produced by some superior virtue and wisdom *of our own.*"

Perhaps these words are for us today as much as for our forebears a century ago.

Remember Lincoln's prescription: "It behooves us then to humble ourselves, to confess our national sins, and to pray for clemency and forgiveness."

"Yours, O Lord, is the kingdom. You are exalted over all. Wealth and honor come from You; You are the ruler of all things, in Your hands are strength and power to exalt and give strength to all. Now, our God, we give You thanks and praise your glorious name."

— 1 Chronicles 29:12-13

19

The people of God are crucial to the future of America.

Whatever hope our nation has is totally dependent upon the people of God living as the people of God.

Christians have got to be Christian!

Their failure to heed and obey God portends destruction, which is why "… judgment must begin at the house of God… "

As representatives of the Kingdom of God in the world, their failure and sin deprives the world of the purifying, healing, redeeming influence of righteousness.

They are salt that has lost its saltiness.

Abraham's intercession for Sodom illustrates this (Genesis 18:32). For the sake of ten righteous God would have spared the city.

Hence the timeliness of the familiar word from God — "If my people who are called by my name will humble themselves, and pray and seek my face, and turn from their wicked ways, then will I hear from heaven, and will forgive their sin and heal their land."

— II Chronicles 7:14

Initially the word applied to a special land; the land God had given Israel... and to a special nation — Israel, who were uniquely the people of God in the ancient world.

But the principle is timeless.

If God's people today will hear and obey, they may expect the response from God which He has promised.

If they refuse and continue in a self-indulgent disregard for justice, America has no hope.

God waits for His people to repent, to pray, to turn from their wicked ways and seek His face.

"Seek ye first the kingdom of God and His righteousness."

— Matthew 6:33

Democracy is not a *numbers game!*

Quality counts as well as quantity.

If a thing is right, ten thousand saying it does not make it more right.

And if a thing is wrong, *ten thousand saying it is right will not make it so!*

A good leader does not count opinion… he weighs it!

The trustworthy elected official is not the one who capitulates to numbers.

True, he is elected to represent his constituency… but he certainly is not a trusted representative if he yields to their pressure when he believes they are wrong.

Our republic *desperately* needs leaders who dare to do what they believe to be true and right and just — no matter how many oppose them.

We urgently need leaders who dare to tell us what we need to hear — not what we want to hear.

The majority can be wrong... and *we do not promote true democracy if we ignore the minority* — even a minority of one!

God give us men and women who have the courage to take political risks, who dare to do the unpopular thing, who follow the way they believe to be the way of justice and truth.

Deliver us from those whose decisions are always expedient and political, never principled.

"And I sought for a man among them who should build up the wall and stand in the gap before me for the land, that I should not destroy it... but I found none."

— Ezekiel 22:30

Recently, a long-time friend who has lived in Europe for thirty years was in Washington.

He had made visits to every section of our country.

His deepest, strongest impression? *The incredible affluence in America,* far exceeding anything with which he was familiar in Europe. Especially noted were the young folk who have been so eminently successful in the past ten years, acquiring small fortunes.

This has been my experience in traveling more than 2 million miles while visiting every continent in the past twenty years.

The wealth in the U.S.A. and the breadth of its distribution is absolutely fantastic — incomprehensible to most non-Americans. Presumption on our part under these circumstances is exceedingly perilous!

Our affluence is not a reason for guilt, but for gratitude... yet a Biblical warning is in order:

"Take heed lest you forget the Lord your God... lest, when you have eaten and are full, and have built goodly houses and live in them...

"And when your herds and flocks multiply, and your silver and gold is multiplied, and all that you have is multiplied — then your heart be lifted up, and you forget the Lord your God...

"Beware lest you say in your heart, 'My power and the might of my hand have gotten me this wealth.'

"You shall remember the Lord your God, for it is He Who gives you power to get wealth.

"And if you forget the Lord your God and go after other gods and serve them and worship them, I solemnly warn you this day that you shall surely perish."

— *Deuteronomy 8:11-14, 17-19*

The U.S.A. didn't just happen... It was ordained of God!

The roots of our unprecedented growth, industry and prosperity as a nation are Biblical roots.

Our way of life sprang from a theology grounded in Judeo-Christian beliefs and values.

Man originated by the creative act of God... He was the crowning glory of God's creation, made in the Divine image.

He was created to be a *partner with God* in the government of the earth by covenant.

He was to increase on the earth, subdue it, keep it and have dominion over it.

He was created to be God's steward, entrusted with the earth in all its incredible productive potential, and he was to be accountable to God in his disposition of this trust.

All this was implicit in the beliefs of those who sought the freedom of America's shores and who shaped a nation in that freedom.

It ought to be obvious to any thoughtful person that *to reject the root is to sacrifice the fruit!*

If belief in God is rejected, the covenant is rejected. If the covenant is rejected, the accountability is rejected...

And if the accountability is rejected, man is operating against reality and futility is inevitable!

Having abandoned the root, we are losing the fruit! That is America's impasse socially, economically and politically!

"So God created man in His own image, in the image of God He created him, male and female He created them. And God blessed them, and God said to them, Be fruitful and multiply, and fill the earth and subdue it; and have dominion over the fish of the sea and over the birds of the air and over every living thing *that* moves upon the earth."

— *Genesis 1:27-28*

Take a look at a profile of our contemporary culture.

In the wisdom of Proverbs, it is stated: "Righteousness exalteth a nation, but sin is a reproach to any people" (Proverbs 14:34).

We are fast becoming a no fault society: no fault insurance — no fault divorce — no fault choice... in effect, a "no fault democracy," which is a contradiction in terms!

Implicit in democracy is order — individual as well as corporate discipline.

Democracy without order is anarchy — and anarchy breeds chaos and tyranny!

We demand freedom without restraint, rights without responsibility, choice without consequences, pleasure without pain.

In our narcissistic, hedonistic, masochistic, valueless preoccupation, we are becoming a people dominated by lust, avarice and greed.

We demand the right to sin but deny the right to train in righteousness… demand the right to oppose religion but deny the right to propagate religion.

In the name of pluralism we demand a distinctiveless, monotonous, meaningless syncretism in which morality is ridiculed, and amorality is celebrated.

And with sublime naivete we wonder at the futility of efforts to eliminate crime, drug abuse, alcohol abuse, child abuse, wife abuse, suicide, war (hot or cold) and the absence of peace (within or without).

We promote consumerism, acquisition, accumulation and prosperity, while we "tip the hat" to poverty, hunger, homelessness, disability, and human need all around us.

Is it any wonder we are losing our influence, our leadership in the world?

"Do not conform any longer to the pattern of this world, but be transformed by the renewing of your mind. Then you will be able to test and approve what God's will is; His good, pleasing, and perfect will."

— *Romans 12:2*

⟿ 24 ⟿

Where does the idea of human rights come from?

If humans are a product of evolution, why are not human rights universal?

Why do human rights have no meaning for a Godless government? Why was it possible for Communist leaders to crush human rights with such indifference to the idea?

Why are human rights fundamental to American thinking? To put it another way, where did the concept of a "Bill of Rights" come from? Why did we celebrate the bicentennial of the first ten amendments to the Constitution?

Why is one presumed innocent until he is proven guilty? Why are the laws of evidence so carefully designed to protect the individual — any individual?

Because our founding fathers took God seriously.

They believed humans were created. That the Creator had endowed them with "certain inalienable rights." They believed that the purpose of government was "to secure" those rights, and that government "received its just powers from the consent of the governed."

They believed in people sovereignty, not government sovereignty!

No God, no human rights. No God, no sovereign people. No God, no freedom. And no justice.

Secularism denies God and denies liberty and justice. And unless America begins to forsake secularism and take God seriously, America will lose everything it holds dear!

"The Lord warned Israel and Judah through all His prophets and seers: 'Turn from your evil ways. Observe my commands and decrees, in accordance with the entire Law that I commanded your fathers to obey and that I delivered to you through my servants the prophets.' "

— *2 Kings 17:13*

Sure we believe in freedom of speech.

You have the power to say what you think... you may even libel another... if you care to take the risk.

(Bear in mind that language can be destructive — it may be a type of violence.)

You've got the right to say anything you like...

But others don't have to listen. They have as much right not to listen as you have to say what you please.

Others are under no obligation to tune you in... and may tune you out any time they wish.

The right to speak is guaranteed...

But you must earn the right to be listened to!

The right to be heard depends solely upon the integrity of the speaker, not upon the obligation of the listener.

Demand your right to speak… but allow another his right not to listen.

To be heard is not a right… it is a responsibility.

Integrity is prerequisite to acceptance.

If you expect to be paid attention to… back it up with your life… let your walk correspond with your talk.

This is fundamental to one's witness for Christ.

Many so-called Christians talk too much, listen too little, and live lives that contradict their speech.

Their "witness" betrays Christ… and alienates those to whom they speak.

Jesus said, "Why do you call me Lord and do not the things I say?"

— Luke 6:46

26

America faces a profound moral issue…

Whether or not to use the incalculable destructive power which science and technology have provided in unlocking the secrets of the atom.

Having created the nuclear bomb, *do we have the moral right to use it?* Having discovered the power, are we obligated to use it?

Are we not under the moral obligation not to do so?

Are we not under a moral mandate to question, to challenge the use of this power?

The issue: the choice is between life and death!

God speaks:

"See, I have set before thee this day life and good, and death and evil; in that I command Thee this day to love the Lord thy God, to walk in His ways, and to keep His commandments and His statutes and His judgments, that thou mayest live.

"But if thine heart turn away, so that thou wilt not hear, but shalt be drawn away, and worship other gods, and serve them...

"I denounce unto you this day, that ye shall surely perish...

"I call heaven and earth to record this day against you, that I have set before you life and death, blessing and cursing: therefore choose life...."

— Deuteronomy 30:15-19

The words were directed to Israel in a specific situation... but the principle involved is certainly relevant to our situation today.

"He that hath ears to hear, let him hear!"

— Matthew 11:15

27

The way of the kingdom of God is antithetical to the way of our contemporary culture.

Our culture says, "Blessed are those who've got it together - who've made it... blessed are the achievers." Jesus said, "Blessed are the poor in spirit."

Our culture says, "Blessed are those who couldn't care less — who are on top... who promote self." Jesus said, "Blessed are those who mourn."

Our culture says, "Blessed are the mighty — the powerful... flaunt it." Jesus said, "Blessed are the meek."

Our culture says, "Blessed are those who are not restrained by moral and ethical taboos... live it up." Jesus said, "Blessed are those who hunger and thirst after righteousness."

Our culture says, "Blessed are the manipulators — the oppressors — the influential." Jesus said, "Blessed are the merciful."

Our culture says, "Blessed are those who, if it feels good, do it." Jesus said, "Blessed are the pure in heart."

Our culture says, "Blessed are the strong — the drivers... the makers and doers." Jesus said, "Blessed are the peacemakers."

Our culture says, "Blessed are the expedient... the compromiser... the conformist... the one who doesn't rock the boat." Jesus said, "Blessed are those who are persecuted for righteousness sake."

Our culture says, "Blessed are those who exercise authority — who lord it over others."

Jesus said, "It shall not be so among you; but whoever would be first among you must be your servant."

— Matthew 20:25

28

What is responsible for America? What has made possible this way of life so greatly cherished? America is not an accident. Who is responsible?

Emerson said that every great law we have comes from the Ten Commandments and the Sermon on the Mount. *Christianity is the root of America.* The church, the Bible, the Gospel… these made our way of life possible.

Free enterprise, private ownership of property, the Bill of Rights, the dignity of man, the immeasurable worth of the individual — *these rise out of the Scriptures!*

Cut a plant from its roots and it will die. An orchid corsage is beautiful and delicate, but it's dead. It's been clipped from its roots. It can be kept in a refrigerator for a time, but eventually it wilts and is thrown out.

Western civilization has been slowly wilting. When it repudiated the church and the Bible, *at that moment it cut itself off from its roots.* That moment disintegration set in, and it began to die.

Decay accelerated until it erupted in two world wars within a quarter century. Then came the atom bomb, Korea, Viet Nam, the Cold War… what next? We try to be optimistic, but our optimism is shallow and tinged with regret.

No nation prospers for long when it forsakes God. Ours is no exception. *God does not want our patronage; He demands our obedience.*

"Woe to those who rise early in the morning to run after their drinks, who stay up late at night till they are inflamed with wine. They have harps and lyres at their banquets, tambourines and flutes and wine, but they have no regard for the deeds of the Lord, no respect for the work of His hands. Therefore my people will go into exile for lack of understanding; their men of rank will die of hunger and their masses will be parched with thirst. Therefore the grave enlarges its appetite and opens its mouth without limit; into it will descend their nobles and masses, with all their brawlers and revelers. Both low and high will be humbled, and the eyes of the arrogant will be brought low, but the Lord Almighty will be exalted by His justice, and the Holy God will show Himself holy by His righteousness."

— *Isaiah 5:11-16*

29

Two voices from the past are tragically relevant…

"Military alliances, balances of power, leagues of nations, all in turn have failed, leaving the only path to be by way of the crucible of war.

"The utter destructiveness of war now blocks out this alternative. We have had our last chance. If we will not devise some greater and more equitable system, Armageddon will be at our door.

"The problem basically is theological and involves a spiritual recrudescence and improvement of human character that will synchronize with our almost matchless advance in science, art, literature and all material and cultural developments of the past two thousand years.

"It must be of the spirit if we are to save the flesh."

— General of the Army Douglas MacArthur at Japanese surrender

"It is a temporary answer to the threat of the world disturbance that we face. The North Atlantic Treaty is temporary. The United Nations is temporary. All our alliances are temporary.

"Basically, there is only one permanence we can all accept. It is the permanence of a God-governed world.

"For the power of God alone is permanent.

"Obedience to His laws is the only road to lasting solutions of man's problems."

— David Lawrence, *U. S. News and World Report* , May 5, 1956

The Scriptures tell us, "Except the Lord build the house, they labor in vain who build...

"Except the Lord keep the city, the watchman waiteth in vain."

— Psalm 127:1

— 30 —

In 1863, President Lincoln designated Thursday, April 30, as a day for National Humiliation, Fasting and Prayer.

In his proclamation, he declared:

"It is the duty of nations as well as of men to owe their dependence upon the overruling power of God.

"… to confess their sins and transgressions in humble sorrow, yet with assured hope that genuine repentance will lead to mercy and pardon.

"… and to recognize the sublime truth announced in the Holy Scriptures and proven by all history, that those nations only are blessed whose God is the Lord.

"… The awful calamity of civil war which now desolates the land may be but a punishment inflicted upon us for our presumptuous sins, to the needful end of our national reformation as a whole people.

"… intoxicated with unbroken success, we have become too self-sufficient to feel the necessity of redeeming and preserving grace, too proud to pray to the God that made us.

"We have grown in numbers, wealth, and power as no other nation has grown — but we have forgotten God.

"We have forgotten the gracious hand that preserved us in peace, and multiplied and enriched and strengthened us.

"We have vainly imagined that all these blessings were produced by some superior virtue and wisdom of our own.

"It behooves us, then, to humble ourselves, to confess our national sins, and to pray for clemency and forgiveness."

The words of President Lincoln echo clearly down the halls of history.

"Do not be anxious about anything, but in everything, by prayer and petition, with thanksgiving, present your requests to God. The peace of God, which transcends all understanding, will guard your hearts and your minds in Christ Jesus."

— *Philippians 4:6,7*

⸺ 31 ⸺

arly in the 19th century the French statesman, Alexander de Tocqueville, made a study of democracy in our country and wrote as follows...

"I sought for the greatness and genius of America in her commodious harbors and her ample rivers, and it was not there.

"I sought for the greatness and genius of America in her fertile fields and boundless forests, and it was not there.

"I sought for the greatness and genius of America in her rich mines and her vast world commerce, and it was not there.

"I sought for the greatness and genius of America in her public school system and her institutions of learning, and it was not there.

"I sought for the greatness and genius of America in her democratic congress and her matchless constitution, and it was not there.

"Not until I went into the churches of America and heard her pulpits flame with righteousness did I understand the secret of her genius and power.

"America is great because America is good, and if America ever ceases to be good, America will cease to be great."

"Righteousness exalts a nation, but sin is a reproach to any people."

— Proverbs 14:34

32

Rome tolerated nearly all religions. The powerful empire took pride in her toleration.

Significantly, there were two exceptions…

Judaism and those who followed *the way of Christ*.

Somehow, Rome's religious pluralism found Biblical faith — Old and New Testament — undesirable.

Caesar was to be worshiped…

Which apparently was not a problem to other religions.

But it was impossible for the Jews, whose faith was monotheistic — the worship of the God of Abraham, Isaac, Israel, Moses and the prophets.

The God, incidentally, of Jesus Christ and his followers.

For them, the God of the Bible exclusively was worthy to be worshiped.

Secularization is moving America in that direction, shoving faith out of public life and into private ghettos.

Somehow today those who name the name of Christ are being discriminated against like the believers in early Rome who finally were forced into the catacombs.

"If the world hates you, keep in mind that it hated me first. If you belonged to the world, it would love you as its own. As it is, you do not belong to the world, but I have chosen you out of the world. That is why the world hates you. Remember the words I spoke to you: 'No servant is greater than his master.' If they persecuted me, they will persecute you also. If they obeyed my teaching, they will obey yours also. They will treat you this way because of my name, for they do not know the one who sent me."

— *John 15:18-21*

33

Fundamental to our contemporary national dilemma is this:

We operate like Marxists, while we attempt to sustain systems rooted in beliefs diametrically opposite!

We reject supernaturalism, accept naturalism and humanism, and try to preserve the fruit of which belief in the supernatural is basic.

We reject creationism, ignoring the fact that it is the very foundation stone of our republic.

(Don't we believe that "all men are *created* equal, and that they are endowed by their *Creator* with certain unalienable rights"?)

Human equality, human rights, governments instituted to secure those rights, and government of the people, by the people, and for the people.

These fundamental American concepts derive from the belief in a Creator God!

To argue for human rights from a non-theistic base is to follow a futile course.

Where atheism is policy human rights are meaningless.

Human rights and atheism are a contradiction in terms… except, of course, an intellectual atheism which enjoys the safety of a culture born of Judeo-Christian values.

Suppose the signers of the Declaration of Independence had declared, "We hold these truths to be self-evident, that all men are descended from monkeys"?

There never would have been a Bill of Rights!

There never would have been a U.S.A.!

"In the beginning God created… "

— *Genesis 1:1*

34

I s financial corruption a cause for concern? Absolutely, because it portends the ruin of a nation.

Since the S & L scandals, the problem seems to be escalating…

The Washington Post reported: "Top executives of the nation's leading trader of government bonds, Salomon Brothers, Inc., revealed clear wrongdoing by their firm."

How many bank failures have occurred recently?

In the same issue of the Post, a commentary by Jack Anderson and Dal Van Atta told the sad story of the University of Pittsburgh, where federal auditors "uncovered $528,681 in apparently misspent research money… "

In the name of research, the university bankrolled dinners, gifts and flights on private planes.

The national debt is astronomical. Private debt equals it, and corporate debt *doubles* the national debt.

What's wrong with us? What of our future as a nation?

Moses, the great lawgiver, had the most accurate and precise diagnosis 3500 years ago:

"Beware that thou forget not the Lord thy God... lest when thou hast eaten and art full, and hast built goodly houses, and dwelt therein; and when thy herds and thy flocks multiply; and thy silver and thy gold is multiplied, and all that thou hast is multiplied...

"Then thine heart be lifted up, and thou forget the Lord thy God... But thou shalt remember the Lord thy God: *for it is He that giveth thee power to get wealth...*

"And it shall be, if thou do at all forget the Lord thy God, and walk after other gods, I testify against you this day that ye shall surely perish. As the nations which the Lord destroyeth before your face, so shall ye perish; because ye would not be obedient unto the voice of the Lord your God!"

— *Deuteronomy 8:11-14,18-20*

Does incipient secularism and the rejection of the God of Moses have anything to do with our national decline?

35

Somewhere I read, concerning the renaissance of the 12th century…

It was characterized by the "recovery of classical literature, recovery of Roman law, recovery of Greek science and its Arabic additions, and the recovery of much of Greek philosophy and its application to academic theology."

The twelfth century was described as "an age marked by a new realism about the world of observable nature and about the real events in the chronology of history."

Also, it saw a "new sense of the identity of the individual through romantic love and chivalry."

What a recovery! In literature, in law, in science, in philosophy, in theology and realism.

In light of our disintegrating culture and the emerging of paganistic elements, a renaissance is desperately needed.

Call it spiritual awakening... call it revival. It is absolutely essential!

The key word is *"recovery."*

Recovery of the faith of our fathers, recovery of family and home, recovery of community, recovery of values, recovery of absolutes...

Recovery of transcendent Reality which orients all of life.

Imagine what kind of impact a renaissance like that would have in America today!

"You, O Lord, reign forever; Your throne endures from generation to generation.

Why do you always forget us? Why do you forsake us so long?

Restore us to yourself, O Lord, that we may return;

Renew our days as of old."

— *Lamentations 5:19-21*

36

God is a good economist!

It is we who foul up the law of supply and demand — and generate a growing imbalance which finally brings the whole system to a grinding halt.

With our pride and avarice and greed, *enough is never enough!*

No matter how much he has, the greedy, avaricious man wants more and more and more and more… He ravages the land, pollutes the atmosphere, and contaminates the water with his lust for more.

He is never satisfied when his needs are met .

He demands luxuries, which soon become necessities in his lifestyle as more and more luxury is sought.

With Madison Avenue pandering to his insatiable appetite, he squanders and wastes more than enough to provide for the needs of many who have little or nothing.

Meanwhile, his solution to the problem is to promote zero population growth by whatever means... wholesale abortion, if nothing else works. Which, incidentally, makes it possible for him to indulge recklessly another kind of lust without fear of consequences.

God is long-suffering... *but such prostitution of the natural appetites which He created in man will not go indefinitely unjudged and unpunished.*

Indeed, the present economic plight of the world is clear evidence that God's laws cannot be broken with impunity. God's justice works slowly... but it works!

So what do we do?

We can continue on our lustful, greedy, avaricious way until we self-destruct.

Or we can repent, confess these sins of the flesh, receive God's forgiveness and renewal, repudiate materialism as a way of life, set limits on our appetites, share our plenty with others, and seek to conform to the will of God in our affairs.

"Now the company of those who believed were of one heart and soul, and no one said that any of the things which he possessed was his own, but they had everything in common... There was not a needy person among them."

— *Acts 2:44*

37

Sixty seconds are always a minute. Sixty minutes are always an hour...

Two pints make a quart, four quarts make a gallon, always...

Twelve inches make a foot, three feet a yard, always...

Sixteen ounces make a pound, twenty-two hundred forty pounds make a ton, always.

It would be impossible for a society to exist without such certainties.

How much more, therefore, are moral and ethical standards necessary?

Moral anarchy is totally destructive of the social order...

Which is at the heart of America's many problems today.

Interestingly, the original temptation (Genesis 3) was motivated by a moral decision.

God had said, "You may eat of every tree in the garden with one exception. Do not even touch it, or you die."

"You shall not die," contradicted the Tempter. "Eat this fruit and be like God, knowing good and Evil."

Without God's moral absolute, people act like god and decide what is good and what is evil. They become their own gods.

Under such circumstances, historically, evil becomes good, and good becomes evil. Romans 1:18-32 is the record of social disintegration.

One of the wisest men who ever lived, Solomon, put it this way: "A false balance is abomination to the Lord; but a just weight is his delight."

— Proverbs 11:1

Social decay in America will not go away. It will increase unless and until we have a moral and spiritual awakening.

"Woe to those who call evil good, and good evil.

Who put darkness for light and light for darkness.

Who put bitter for sweet and sweet for bitter."

— Isaiah 5:20

38

There is a growing movement away from the social order in America today, based upon the mistaken belief that freedom is found when there are no rules. Improvisation — not order. License — not restrictive rules. No rules — let everyone do what is right in his own eyes. Some people call it "libertarianism," others "anarchy."

Friends, *order is freedom. Disorder is bondage!*

Moral permissiveness in the name of personal freedom is delusion of the greatest magnitude.

To live on the basis of "I do as I please" is to court disaster.

Imagine a football game without any rules…

It wouldn't last ten minutes! (If anyone would even bother to get involved.)

Imagine a busy intersection downtown without traffic lights…

It would take hours to untangle the tie up.

And the longer it took the worse it would get as tempers were inflamed, people were trying to take matters into their own hands.

You see, *rules make the game.* Thousands enjoy playing the game, and multiplied thousands are thrilled as they watch it.

Rules are as basic to life as they are to games.

American life is governed by a moral order, instituted by God and agreed upon among men.

Man violates that order at his own peril.

Morality is not arbitrary… it is part of the natural law of the universe and as basic to life as gravity.

"For the wages of sin is death, but the gift of God is eternal life through Jesus Christ our Lord."

— Romans 6:23

39

Who speaks for the voiceless?
Who speaks for the powerless?
Who speaks for the poor?
Who speaks for Jesus?

Jesus said, "I was hungry and you gave me something to eat, I was thirsty and you gave me something to drink, I was a stranger and you invited me in, I needed clothes and you clothed me, I was sick and you looked after me, I was in prison and you came to visit me."

— Matthew 25:35-36

They said, "When did we do this?" Jesus said, "Inasmuch as you did it unto the least of these, you did it unto me."

We have reduced justice in America to a legal system, limiting it to judges and courts and attorneys and trials.

In the Bible *justice has to do with providing for the poor, the homeless, the widow, the orphan, and the prisoner.*

Justice is related to compassion…

Justice is expressed in mercy…

Justice is the response of love…

Justice is the way of righteousness.

"Seek justice — Encourage the oppressed. Defend the cause of the fatherless. Plead the cause of the widow."

— Isaiah 1:17

Jesus is hungry — feed Him

Jesus is thirsty — give Him drink.

Jesus is a stranger — invite Him in.

Jesus is naked — clothe Him.

Jesus is sick — visit Him.

Jesus is in prison — go to Him!

40

Americanism may be idolatry!

If I am uncritical of my country, *one very basic ingredient is missing from my allegiance.*

"My country right or wrong" may be the mark of loyalty… or it may betray abdication from personal responsibility.

Blind acceptance of my country's wrongs is as treasonable as collaboration with her enemies.

Either way I am contributing to her destruction!

Romantic, sentimental, childish attitudes toward America do not constitute allegiance.

Mature, critical, constructive attitudes do!

The process whereby romantic acceptance is turned into constructive citizenship is disillusionment.

Just as my childish belief in a Santa Claus who descended the chimney to deliver presents carried in a sleigh drawn by reindeer was dissipated through disillusionment...

So my childish views of American history must be dissolved and replaced by the truth about her faults and failures...

If I am to be a faithful, responsible citizen.

Many of those who professed to believe in the self-evident truth that "all men are created equal and that they are endowed by their creator with certain unalienable rights... " were slave holders...

Who refused to practice what they professed and therefore denied what they said they believed.

True allegiance does not require me to approve such hypocrisy.

Nor does it free me from the obligation to do whatever I can to change the immeasurable evil which has issued from it.

"Rulers are not a terror to good conduct, but to bad... He (the ruler) is the servant of God to execute his wrath on the wrongdoer."

— *Romans 13:3, 4*

ow do you explain our blindness to the connection between God and freedom?

Have we learned nothing from seventy years of Communism?... Did the Soviet Union teach us nothing? China? Eastern Europe? Cuba?

Godlessness and Atheism are totally incompatible with liberty... Godlessness cannot tolerate freedom. *Godliness is the root of freedom.*

To be sure there are those who profess faith in God who would banish freedom for any but themselves... Many religious Americans, many Islamic governments...

And there are many who profess atheism who take freedom seriously, but they reflect the culture in which they have been reared — while they reject the roots of that culture: Judeo-Christian (Biblical) values.

They hold our forefathers' vision but reject their faith in God, which is the basis of their view of government!

While they advocate freedom, they diminish it, reducing it to anarchy, eliminating all values, forsaking law and order for doing as one pleases.

Godlessness inevitably abandons order, moral and ethical standards, as all rules become relative and ethics situational.

The fact is that our culture has degenerated to the place where wealth and pleasure (instant gratification) and security have become our gods. With the result that we are a valueless society with, thank God, some glorious exceptions, but generally secular.

The cry of the Minutemen who fought for the freedom and liberty of America in the Revolutionary war was this: "No King but King Jesus!"

As we look to the King of Kings, we find order, morality, and peace. That was God's basis in the founding of America.

"God who gave us life gave us liberty. Can the liberties of a nation be secure if we remove from the hearts of the people the belief that those liberties are the gift of God?"

— Thomas Jefferson

42

I n my years as Chaplain of the Senate, I cannot remember a time of greater frustration among members of Congress and their staffs, or more expressions of anger from the people, than we are currently experiencing.

Several years ago there came to my attention a quote from a book written by Alexander Fraser Tytler, who lived at the end of the 18th century and the early part of the 19th (1748-1813). He wrote a book entitled, *The Decline and Fall of the Athenian Republic.*

Amazing, is it not, that the following quotation from that book, written about ancient democracy, long before American democracy had been really tested, is so timely.

Tytler wrote:

"A democracy cannot exist as a permanent form of government. It can only exist until the voters discover that they can vote themselves money from the Public Treasury. From that moment on the majority always votes for the candidates promising the most benefits from the Public Treasury with a result that a democracy always collapses over loose fiscal policy always followed by dictatorship.

The average age of the world's greatest civilizations has been 200 years. These nations have progressed through the following sequence:

From bondage to spiritual faith;

    from spiritual faith to great courage;

        from courage to liberty;

            from liberty to abundance;

                from abundance to selfishness;

from selfishness to complacency;

    from complacency to apathy;

        from apathy to dependency;

            from dependency back into bondage."

"Blessed is the nation whose God is the Lord."

— Psalm 33:12

43

After forty years in Washington, involved with the prayer breakfast movement, plus thirty years as a pastor and more than ten years as Senate chaplain...

I have growing impression — a deepening conviction...

The greatest single reason for failure in government, to the extent it has failed... and the progressive secularization of our culture with corresponding social decay...

Is the prayerlessness of the people of God!

Paul, the apostle, instructing a young pastor, advised him that prayer was a matter of first importance...

"First of all, I urge that supplication, prayers, intercessions, and thanksgivings be made for all people, for kings and all who are in high positions..."

— I Timothy 2:1-2

To which he attached two significant benefits...

1. A desirable social condition: "... that we may lead *a quiet and peaceable life*, godly and respectful in every way."

2. Effective outreach: "This is good and acceptable in the sight of God our Savior, *who desires all to be saved* and to come to a knowledge of the truth."

When God's people take prayer seriously and intercede with thanksgiving for all people and for all in authority...

We may live in peace and quietness — godly and reverent.

And evangelism and mission will flourish.

What a mandate for our time — faithful in prayer!

What a prospect for life and mission!

"Be joyful always. Pray without ceasing. Give thanks is all circumstances, for this is God's will for you in Christ Jesus."

— *1 Thessalonians 5:17*

44

The descent of a disintegrating culture:

Rejection of God: "Because that, when they knew God, they glorified him not as God, neither were thankful; but became vain in their imaginations, and their foolish heart was darkened."

— *Romans 1:21*

Distorted thinking: "Professing themselves to be wise, they became fools… "

— *Romans 1:22*

False worship: "… And changed the glory of the incorruptible God into an image made like to corruptible man, and to birds, and fourfooted beasts, and creeping things."

— *Romans 1:23*

Inevitable consequences: "Wherefore God also gave them up to uncleanness through the lusts of their own hearts, to dishonor their own bodies between themselves; Who changed the truth of God into a lie, and worshiped and served the creature more than the Creator, who is blessed for ever. Amen."

— *Romans 1:24-25*

Perversion: "And even as they did not like to retain God in their knowledge, God gave them over to a reprobate mind, to do those things which are not convenient; Being filled with all unrighteousness, fornication, wickedness, covetousness, maliciousness; full of envy, murder, debate, deceit, malignity; whisperers, backbiters, haters of God, despiteful, proud, boasters, inventors of evil things, disobedient to parents. Without understanding, covenant-breakers, without natural affection, implacable, unmerciful: Who knowing the judgment of God, that they which commit such things are worthy of death, not only do the same, but have pleasure in them that do them."

— Romans 1:28-32

The way back: "For when we were yet without strength, in due time Christ died for the ungodly. For scarcely for a righteous man will one die; yet peradventure for a good man some would even dare to die. But God commendeth his love toward us, in that, while we were yet sinners, Christ died for us. Much more then, being now justified by his blood, we shall be saved from wrath through him. For if, when we were enemies, we were reconciled to God by the death of his Son, much more, being reconciled, we shall be saved by his life."

— Romans 5:6-10

God loves us and offers us His salvation... what good news!

45

The fear of the Lord is the beginning of knowledge... "

— Proverbs 1:7

Those words are the product of one of the wisest men who ever lived — King Solomon.

In our secularized society, very few would agree. But let's get philosophical for a moment...

Suppose we were led by One Who was perfect in love, perfect in righteousness and justice, perfectly equitable, perfectly wise...

And suppose such leadership motivated everyone in our society to emulate such a Leader...

A society where perfect love, perfect righteousness and justice, perfect equity, perfect wisdom would prevail.

Can you imagine a better social order?

As a matter of fact, the God of the Bible is portrayed as perfect in all these attributes.

What if He were feared (reverenced) by every person in our society?

Would that not be an ideal social order?

Can you imagine a wiser way to organize society?

Read the words of the first Americans, those pilgrims who arrived aboard the *Mayflower* and committed themselves to this compact:

"Having undertaken, *for the glory of God and advancement of the Christian Faith* and honor of our King and country, a voyage to plant the first colony in the northern parts of Virginia, do by these presents solemnly and mutually in the presence of God and one of another, *covenant and combine ourselves together into a civil body politic, for our better ordering and preservation and furtherance of the ends aforesaid,* and by virtue hereof to enact, constitute and frame such just and equal laws, ordinances, acts, constitutions and offices from time to time, as shall be thought most meet and convenient for the general good of the colony. Unto which we promise all due submission and obedience."

oses warned Israel of the *peril in prosperity* 3500 years ago:

"Take heed lest you forget the Lord your God...

"Lest, when you have eaten and are full, and have built goodly houses and live in them, and when your herds and flocks multiply and your silver and gold is multiplied, and all that you have is multiplied...

"Then your heart be lifted up, and you forget the Lord your God...

"Beware lest you say in your heart, 'My power and the might of my hand have gotten me this wealth.'...

"You shall remember the Lord your God, for it is he who gives you the power to get wealth...

"And if you forget the Lord your God and go after other gods and serve them and worship them, I solemnly warn you this day that you shall surely perish.

"Like the nations that the Lord makes to perish before you, so shall you perish...

"Because you would not obey the voice of the Lord your God."

— Deuteronomy 8:11-14, 17-20

What do you put your *trust* in?

What do you put your *hope* in?

"The world and its desires pass away, but the man who does the will of God lives forever."

— 1 John 2:17

47

An insight into our present American culture:

Two thirds of the front page of the "Style" section of the Washington Post — one of America's most respected and influential papers...

A portion of a steel and concrete monstrosity, titled in part, "the spirit of concrete space."

Subtitle: "back-to-basic beauty"!?

The architect's explanation: "My intention is to create a spiritual world, to make space so strong and deep it will penetrate to the people who contact that space."

And the Washington Post took it seriously!

Incidentally — same page — less than one column on the wedding of President Kennedy's daughter.

A wedding where people gathered *"in the presence of God"* and made vows *to God and to each other.*

So much for contemporary understanding of *"spiritual."*

Did the editors mean it as a joke...

Or is this where some American journalism is at the end of the twentieth century???

Why doesn't our major media depict Christian Americans in a positive, healthy light?

Why is the father always portrayed as a fool, the pastor as a secret sinner, and the Christian as the hypocritical bigot?

St. Paul, the apostle, speaks with penetrating wisdom...

"Claiming to be wise they became fools."

— *Romans 1:22-24*

48

I n three vivid, brief statements:

The graphic and tragic end of one powerful ruler…

Uzziah, King of Judah for fifty-two years…

The record of the destructive peril in power…

 It has never been more timely than now!

"… as his power increased

his heart grew proud…

and this was his ruin!"

— *II Chronicles 26:16*

The inevitable course of secularism.

The biography of one who is his own god!

Do you remember the words of our Puritan forefathers?

"We give up our selves unto that God whose name is Jehovah, and unto our blessed Lord Jesus Christ, promising, by the help of His Spirit and grace, to cleave unto Him… by faith in a way of Gospel obedience, as becometh His covenant people forever. We also give up our offspring unto God in Jesus Christ, avouching the Lord to be our God, and the God of our children, and our selves, with our children to be His people, humbly adoring this grace of God, that we and our offspring with us, may be looked upon as the Lord's. We do also give up our selves one unto another in the Lord, and according to the will of God, freely covenanting and binding our selves to walk together as a right ordered congregation and church of Christ, in all ways of His worship, according to the holy rules of the Word of God, promising brotherly love, faithfully to watch over one another's souls."

49

Much concern is being expressed these days about failure in public education in America.

All sorts of remedies are being proposed…

But it never seems to occur to those concerned that *the disintegration of public education corresponds to the secularization of education.*

There seems to be a rather direct correlation.

As a case in point, examine the Christian private schools — elementary, secondary, colleges and universities…

There is no lack of quality education there!

As these private schools have proliferated, there has been no breakdown of excellence…

If anything, it has been the opposite.

This is not a prayer-in-the-schools issue!

It is a case of the deliberate secularization of life.

Transvaluation of fundamental values which are the strength of our way of life at its best.

Indifference to, if not direct rejection of, the Judeo-Christian roots of our Republic.

Translating evil into positive good…

Absolutizing the relative and relativizing absolutes!

The second Psalm tells the story…

"Why do the nations conspire, and the people plot in vain? The kings of the earth set themselves, and the rulers take counsel together against the Lord and his anointed, saying, 'Let us burst their bonds asunder, and cast their cords from us.'"

For education to be strong, it must be built on a strong foundation…

The foundation of absolute truth. The foundation of God in our history.

"For attaining wisdom and discipline; for understanding words of insight; for acquiring a disciplined and prudent life, doing what is right and just and fair… the fear of the Lord is the beginning of knowledge, but fools despise wisdom and discipline."

— Proverbs 1:2,3,7

50

Not a word of the first amendment can be construed as forbidding religious involvement in our political system.

"Congress shall make no law respecting an establishment of religion… "

Nothing ambiguous about that!

"… nor prohibit the free exercise thereof."

Equally clear and explicit!

Now connect the second clause with the subject of the sentence:

"Congress shall make no law… " (which shall) "prohibit the free exercise" (of religion).

The constitution guarantees the "free exercise" of religion…

And prohibits Congress from making any law which circumvents such freedom!

We are hearing a great deal about the first half of the equation, but very little about the second half!

The first amendment, to put it plainly, tells the government to *stay out of religion*.

But it does not prohibit religion from getting involved in government!

Christians have always been involved in the leadership of our country.

It is this very fact that helped make our country great. Spiritual, godly men shaped out country...

Imagine the difference in America if our founding fathers had not believed in God, His Word, or His guidance!

"Politics and religion don't mix" is not a logical deduction from the constitution.

Indeed, the very fact that our founding fathers drafted the 'first amendment was a clear expression of their religious conviction.

The first amendment exists to *protect* our churches from government, not to *exclude* them from government.

"There is no power but of God; the powers that be are ordained of God."

— *Romans 13:1*

ar begets war:

"You have plowed iniquity," wrote the prophet Hosea…

"You have reaped injustice…

"You have eaten the fruit of lies.

"Because you have trusted in your chariots and in the multitude of your warriors…

"Therefore the tumult of war shall arise among your people…

"And all your fortresses shall be destroyed."

Ponder the statement, "… *you have trusted in your chariots.*"

The issue is not just the instruments of war, but also putting one's trust in them.

This is the bottom line of history — where does the man put his trust?

The divine order is trust in God.

Refuse to trust God and all trust will be misplaced.

The man who will not trust in God, who trusts in man and his ingenuity and exploits, will end up trusting neither God nor man.

Failure to orient life around trust in God results in the breakdown of trust everywhere.

It is written large in history that no nation, no empire, no kingdom was ever able to perpetuate itself by depending upon military might.

Our nation is no exception.

On our coins we profess "In God we trust."

When we begin to take seriously that profession, we can begin to look forward to the fruits of peace.

"They that take the sword shall perish by the sword."

— *Matthew 26:52*

od revealed to Father Abraham His plan to destroy Sodom and Gomorrah in judgment in Genesis 18.

Abraham asked God if He would save the city for the sake of fifty righteous.

God said He would.

Abraham lowered the figure — forty five righteous? Forty? Thirty? Twenty?... Ten?

For the sake of ten righteous God said He would save the city.

Where are the righteous in America?

I did not say the religious! We have plenty of them.

Nor the evangelical... nor the conservative... nor the orthodox... nor the fundamentalist...

But the righteous... *where are the righteous?*

Where are those who profess to take Jesus Christ seriously, who conform to what He taught, who follow His life style, who are like Christ in their living?

Where are those who "Seek first the kingdom of God and His righteousness?"

Where are those who "hunger and thirst after righteousness?"

Where are those who not only call Him "Lord," but who do what He says?

America needs you.

"You are the salt of the earth; but if salt has lost its taste, how shall its saltiness be restored? It is no longer good for anything except to be thrown out and trodden under foot by men."

— Matthew 5:13

53

Years ago, a Washington Post reader, responding to the Susan B. Anthony dollar, wrote to the editor reminding him that Anthony was an atheist "who rejected any idea of supernatural interference in human society."

His point: *Susan B. Anthony and the statement, "In God we trust," were a contradiction in terms!*

He went on, "She believed the human race can and must create its own noble destiny and fulfillment, with man and woman, equal and together, the sole source of strength, progress and ideals for its well-being and happiness."

No clearer statement of the religion of humanism could be made.

And it is a precise explanation for the human dilemma at this point in history with its explosion of knowledge and its incredible technological progress…

Despite which, none of the profound social problems which have troubled human history have been solved, but rather have grown worse. War is a prime example.

Way back in 1979 William Greider wrote in the *Washington Post*, "In the early 1970's, when the U.S. began to talk about arms agreements with the Russians, we had about 400 nuclear warheads — enough to obliterate the Soviet Union, people, factories, trees, dogs and bears.

By 1972 when Salt I was signed, we had 3,000 warheads. When Salt II was signed, we had nearly 9,000 warheads. Some estimate we produced over 16,000 by 1990.

The consummate product of our progress is the chief threat to human survival. Even with the demise of the former Soviet Union we cannot claim to have peace in the world. If anything, our world seems more unstable as we wonder who has nuclear weapons, and who might be willing to use them.

The religion of humanism cannot save humanity. Technology and science cannot save humanity. The inner searchings of so-called "new ager's" cannot save humanity.

"Separated from Christ... without hope and without God in the world."

— Ephesians 2:12

"For the creation waits with eager longing for the revealing of the sons of God; for the creation was subjected to futility, not of its own will but by the will of Him who subjected it in hope."

— Romans 8:19-20

54

Either God is... of God is not.

If God is not, then nothing matters anyway.

Humanity will go on doing the best that it can in its fantastic scientific and technological progress, perennially victimized by its own selfishness, failure, and sin.

With all his progress, man keeps refining the instruments of his own destruction.

But if God is...

Then there is hope — even for sinful, hedonistic, selfish mankind.

He loves, He cares, nothing is too hard or impossible for Him.

If God is, either He is in charge of history or He is not.

If He is not, *mankind is without hope.* His aspirations are illusions. Life is irrational and absurd.

But the Bible records the exciting fact that God is in charge of history...

History is really His Story.

History is going somewhere. It has purpose — a consummation!

Life has meaning. Man has destiny.

"For He has made known to us in all wisdom and insight the mystery of His will according to His purpose which He set forth in Christ as a plan for the fullness of time, to unite all things in Him, things in heaven and in earth."

— Ephesians 1:9-10

"We know that in everything God works for good with those who love Him, who are called according to His purpose."

— Romans 8:28

God has a plan for America! God has a plan for you!

55

What is progress? How do you define it? Does it mean change? If so, what kind of change?

Is change from oxen to auto to airplane progress? Is change from slow to fast progress? Are speed and efficiency the criteria of progress?

Has human nature changed? If so, how?

Man's clothes have changed — his food has changed — his toys have changed — his instruments of production have changed — his pleasures have changed…

But has man changed?

He used to kill with bow and arrow — now he kills with atom bombs. He used to travel a few miles an hour — now he exceeds the speed of sound.

To what advantage this saving of time?

(When asked why he did not wish to travel faster, an old Vermont farmer replied, "Because I figure I pass up more than I catch up with.")

Crime has not lessened. Suicide has not lessened. Divorce has not lessened. Drug abuse has not lessened. Alcoholism has not lessened.

Avarice — greed - pride — jealousy — lust — gluttony have not lessened!

Where's our progress?

Progress requires a legitimate end... and in our culture all our ends are means.

Individually or collectively we have no legitimate - no ultimate goal... and many of our systems and institutions have become diabolical and destructive.

"Although they knew God they did not honor Him as God or give thanks to Him, but they became futile in their thinking and their senseless minds were darkened. Thinking themselves wise, they became fools."

— Romans 1: 21

56

Religious tolerance may be a facade concealing deep intolerance; a cover-up for godlessness by those who have no religious conviction. (Note that I said *conviction* — to believe everything is to believe nothing.)

Historically, those systems whose policy is tolerance of all religion become intolerant of God-fearing people.

Rome, for example, tolerated all religious people, but persecuted Jews and Christians.

Irreligion turns out to be vehement intolerance.

Take for instance some thoughts from a Washington Post article written by Joseph Sobran entitled, *"Homogenizing Children."*

"Many folks of the liberal persuasion are intensely suspicious of any means of public support to private education.

"They regard such means as a devious way of subsidizing Catholicism. Never mind that they want all of us, Catholics included, to subsidize liberalism — right down to the last abortion.

"It is unconstitutional, you know, for Catholics to do to liberals, what liberals do to Catholics.

"Religion is supposed to be excluded from the classroom, on constitutional grounds… anti-religion is not!

"If a teacher preaches Christianity in class, he violates the separation (or is it 'segregation'?) of Church and State.

"But if he mocks religion in the classroom, he is merely exercising his academic freedom.

"We forbid the one and subsidize the other. We have established irreligion.'"

There are some religions, some forms of Judaism and Christianity, which practice intolerance of those who differ… but such an attitude is indefensible on the grounds of the Bible.

The Bible clearly teaches God's love for all — even those who reject Him. True biblical faith promotes respect and love for those who hold different views: "You shall love your neighbor as yourself."

— *Leviticus 19:18*

"Love is the fulfilling of the law."

— *Romans 13:10*

57

A prophetic utterance from out of the past... an editorial from April, 1949:

"The greatest threat to our civilization comes from within that civilization itself: secularism.

A much blunter word is *godlessness*.

Our civilization, for all its churches and all its churchgoers, is predominantly a secular, godless civilization."

Which is why the problems we face as human beings do not yield to all the effort and money and expertise we expend to solve them.

The root of the matter is man's self-alienation from God.

Seduced by the religion of humanism — which incidentally was the original temptation in the Garden of Eden — man refuses to acknowledge his need of and submission to God.

Abraham Lincoln said it perfectly in his proclamation designating April 30, 1863, as a day of national humiliation and prayer:

"Intoxicated with unbroken success, we have become too self-sufficient to feel the necessity of redeeming and preserving grace, too proud to pray to the God that made us.

"We have grown in numbers, wealth and power as no other nation has grown — but we have forgotten God.

"We have forgotten the gracious hand that preserved us in peace, and multiplied and enriched and strengthened us...

"We have vainly imagined that all these blessings were produced by some superior virtue and wisdom of our own. *It behooves us then, to humble ourselves, to confess our national sins, and to pray for clemency and forgiveness.*"

"If my people who are called by my name humble themselves, and pray and seek my face, and turn from their wicked ways, then I will hear from heaven, and will forgive their sin and heal their land."

— *II Chronicles 7:14*

The United States is a military power... and yet...

Military strength alone does not guarantee national security.

Moral and spiritual strength is essential!

History is replete with evidence that no great empire was defeated from without before it had disintegrated spiritually, morally, and ethically within.

The Roman Empire certainly did not collapse for lack of military power.

Rome was fatally vulnerable to the fierce forces from without because of its materialism, its hedonism, its self-indulgence, its amoral social decay within.

America, the strongest nation in history, will not be destroyed by forces from without but *from its own decadence.*

Secularism — materialism — hedonism — self indulgence — immorality — sexual permissiveness — drunkenness — drug abuse — these are like a cancer ravaging America's health and strength.

The need is critical for the people to take a stand against those conditions which are contributing to the pollution, corruption, and moral decay of American life.

It is time for Christians to take a stand for morality, decency, and righteousness.

There is the story of the little boy who, when the hall clock chimed thirteen, came running excitedly into his mother's bedroom, shouting, "Mommy, Mommy, it's later than it has ever been before."

It is!

Jesus answered them, "When it is evening, you say, 'It will be fair weather; for the sky is red.' And in the morning, 'It will be stormy today, for the sky is red and threatening.' You know how to interpret the appearance of the sky, but you cannot interpret the signs of the times."

— *Matthew 16:2-3*

What characterized the culture of Isaiah's day?

Materialism — "Woe to you who add house to house and join field to field until there is no space left, and you live alone in the land."

Hedonism — "Woe to those who rise early in the morning to run after drinks, who stay up late at night till they are inflamed with wine."

Defiance — "Woe to those who draw sin along with cords of deceit… to those who say, 'Let God hurry, let Him hasten His work so we may see it. Let it approach, let the plan of the Holy One of Israel come, so we may know it."

Perversion — "Woe to those who call evil good, and good evil."

Arrogance — "Woe to those who are wise in their own eyes and clever in their own sight."

Corruption — "Woe to those… who acquit the guilty for a bribe, but deny justice to the innocent."

And what was the result? "Therefore as tongues of fire lick up straw and as dry grass sinks down in the flame, so their roots will decay and their flowers blow away like dust; for they have rejected the law of the Lord Almighty and spurned the word of the Holy One of Israel."

— Isaiah 5:8, 11, 18, 20, 21-24

In the last half century secularism has been growing and deepening in our culture.

Speaking through the prophet Jeremiah, the Lord God said: "What wrong did your fathers find in me that they went far from me, and went after worthlessness?"

"... and became worthless!"

— Jeremiah 2:5

"For my people have committed two evils: they have forsaken me, the fountain of living waters, and hewed out cisterns for themselves... broken cisterns that can hold no water."

American society is corrupted with the same characteristics as that of Isaiah and Jeremiah. God is calling us to return to Himself, before the same fate arrives.

⟞ 60 ⟝

It was in a time of crisis…

A time when the nation was at war…

Some of his closest advisors were turning against him…

When President Lincoln found solace in the words to a hymn written by poet and abolitionist Julia Ward Howe after visiting the soldier's camp outside of Washington.

"Mine eyes have seen the glory of the coming of the Lord,

He is trampling out the vintage where the grapes of wrath are stored,

He hath loosed the fateful lightning of His terrible swift sword,

His truth is marching on.

I have seen Him in the watchfires of a hundred circling camps,

They have builded Him an altar in the evening dews and damps,

I can read His righteous sentence by the dim and flaring lamps;

His day is marching on.

He has sounded forth the trumpet that shall never sound retreat,

He is sifting out the hearts of men before His judgment seat,

O be swift, my soul, to answer Him, be jubilant, me feet!

Our God is marching on.

In the beauty of the lilies, Christ was born across the sea,

With a glory in His bosom that transfigures you and me,

As He died to make men holy, let us die to make men free

While God is marching on."

Look at those words… the courage of conviction… the sureness of the cause… the commitment to the task… the willingness to battle… the recognition that each soldier was willing to die for the cause.

Those words moved a nation. May they inspire us as we recognize the work to which God has called America.